Black Is...

By

Mia Morton Hubbard

Published by

Queen V Publishing

Englewood, OH

QueenVPublishing.com

Published by
Queen V Publishing
Englewood, OH
QueenVPublishing.com

Copyright © 2024 by Mia Morton Hubbard

All rights reserved. No part of this book may be reproduced or transmitted in any form or by any means, electronic or mechanical, without prior written consent of the author, except for the inclusion of brief quotes in a review.

Library of Congress Control Number: 2024906733

ISBN-13: 978-1-7358162-2-7

Cover design and illustrations by Vladimir Cebu, LL.B.

Edited by Valerie J. Lewis Coleman of Pen of the Writer and Keitorria Edmonds of The Final Edit Co

Printed in the United States

This book belongs to

_____

Grandma, what is black?

That's a good question. Let's see...

Black is...

The color of night
that makes the stars shine so bright.
Oh, what a beautiful sight.

Black is...

The stallion that rides with the wind.
Faster and faster, again and again.

The butterfly landing on colorful flowers, having fun for hours and hours.

Black is...

The bird that flies high in the air, gathering worms for her babies to share.

The bear that loves her cubs.

She snuggles with them and gives them rubs.

The baby panther that loves his mommy so much, needing and wanting her special touch.

Black is...

A bunch of grapes that are juicy and yummy.
Eat them one-by-one to fill your tummy.

Black is...

The dress Mommy wears on a date with Daddy, eating, dancing, and feeling happy.

he 44th President of the United States, Mr. Barack Obama.
He looks like you, your sister, Daddy, and Momma.

Black is...

My grandson who's beautiful inside and out.
My love for you makes me want to shout!

Since a child's view of color affects how they see the world, Mia Morton Hubbard encourages children to love themselves as they are and give that same love to others.

Mrs. Mia is available to speak to your children about career opportunities and setting goals to achieve them. Connect with her at MiaMortonHubbard.com.

For bulk purchases of Black Is..., multicultural crayons, activities, and complimentary coloring sketches, visit BlackIsTheBook.com.

SCAN ME

www.ingramcontent.com/pod-product-compliance
Lightning Source LLC
Chambersburg PA
CBHW041524070526
44585CB00002B/68